2-97-3

Everyday English

Book 4
Second Edition

Everyday English

Book 4
Second Edition

Barbara Zaffran
Staff Development Specialist in
ESL and Native Languages
New York City

David Krulik
Former Director
Secondary-School ESL Programs
New York City

Consulting Editor
Linda Schinke-Llano, Ph.D.

National Textbook Company
NTC a division of *NTC Publishing Group* • Lincolnwood, Illinois USA

*To Alain, with love
and remembrance*

Cover Photo Credits: Camerique (bottom left);
T. Dietrich/H. Armstrong Roberts (bottom right);
©Brent Jones (top left); J. Parkinson/H. Armstrong
Roberts (top right)

1996 Printing

Published by National Textbook Company, a division of NTC Publishing Group.
©1991 by NTC Publishing Group, 4255 West Touhy Avenue,
Lincolnwood (Chicago), Illinois 60646-1975 U.S.A.
6 7 8 9 VP 9 8 7

Contents

Unit 1 Feelings and Emotions

Lesson 1   **Emotions**

Exercise 1   Study these emotions.

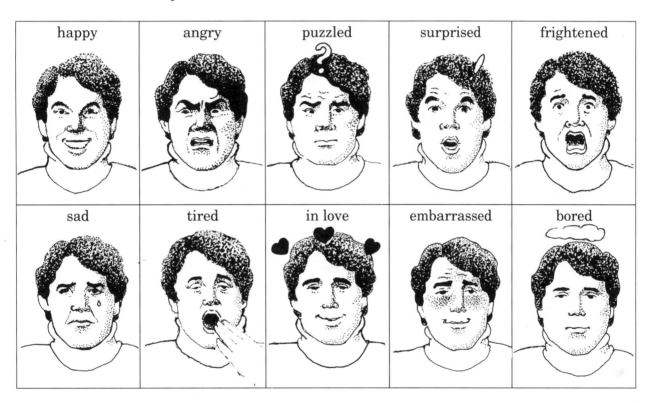

Exercise 2   Use your dictionary to help you find out about these emotions. Write their meanings on the lines provided.

anxious (worried) _____

_____

guilty _____

_____

disappointed _____

_____

hurt _____

_____

excited _____

_____

jealous _____

_____

frustrated _____

_____

nervous _____

_____

bored _____

_____

annoyed _____

_____

Exercise 3   Match each face with an emotion. Write the correct word for each picture on the line.

angry   happy   sad   frightened   tired

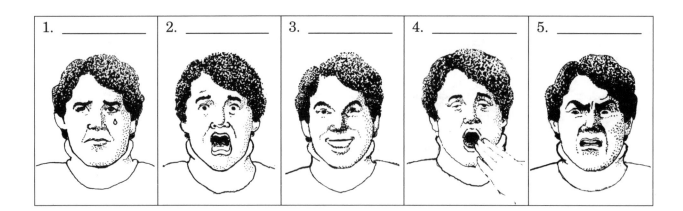

Exercise 4   Antonyms are words that have opposite meanings. Match the antonyms. Write the correct letter on the line next to each number.

_____ 1. nervous

a. interested

_____ 2. bored

b. satisfied

_____ 3. happy

c. tolerant

_____ 4. jealous

d. calm

_____ 5. frustrated

e. sad

_____ 6. tired

f. sure

_____ 7. embarrassed

g. proud

_____ 8. guilty

h. awake

_____ 9. puzzled

i. innocent

Exercise 5   Synonyms are words that have about the same meaning. Circle the synonym for the word at the left.

1. annoyed   a. excited   b. bothered   c. bored

2. worried   a. anxious   b. excited   c. guilty

3. surprised   a. bored   b. sad   c. startled

4. angry   a. hungry   b. mad   c. hot

5. frightened   a. brave   b. scared   c. silly

6. happy   a. content   b. continent   c. love

7. sad   a. bored   b. unhappy   c. embarrassed

8. puzzled   a. tired   b. annoyed   c. confused

9. tired   a. sleepy   b. calm   c. relaxed

10. hurt   a. embarrassed   b. jealous   c. offended

Exercise 6   Choose the correct word, and write it on the line to complete each sentence.

1. He is a _____ person.
(jealous / jealousy)

2. When I am mad, I am _____ .
(angry / anger)

3. If I do something wrong, I am _____ .
   (guilty / guilt)

4. I am brave. I am not _____ .
   (fear / frightened)

5. I failed my test. I was very _____ .
   (disappointed / disappointment)

Exercise 7   Write a synonym and an antonym for each of these words.

	Synonym	**Antonym**
1. sad	_____	_____
2. happy	_____	_____
3. frightened	_____	_____
4. puzzled	_____	_____
5. tired	_____	_____

Lesson 2   Situations

Exercise 1   Answer the questions in complete sentences.

1. How do you feel when your boyfriend or girlfriend goes away?

   _____

2. How do you feel when your parents don't let you do something you want to do?

   _____

3. How do you feel when your teacher gives you a surprise test?

   _____

4. How do you feel when you leave your homework or your book at home?

   _____

5. How do you feel when your team wins a big game?

   _____

Everyday English, Book Four

Exercise 2   Read the following situations. In small groups, discuss how the people feel. Remember that people can have different emotions in the same situations. Then join with your group to share ideas with the entire class.

1. Liliana and her friends are planning a trip to the beach on Saturday. Saturday comes, and it is raining. Is Liliana happy? Why? How does she feel?

2. Luis and Miguel are playing a game on the computer. Ruben sees them playing, and he asks to play too. But only two people can play the game, not three. How does Ruben feel? How do Luis and Miguel feel?

3. Reiko is looking for a job. She is out shopping, and she sees a "Help Wanted" sign in a store. How does Reiko feel?

4. Peter's favorite group is giving a concert in his town. He goes to a music store to buy tickets. He learns that all the tickets are sold. How does Peter feel?

5. Jayshree is in the library. She is studying for an important test. The two other people at her table are talking to one another. She asks them to stop talking because she wants to study. They continue to talk. How does Jayshree feel? How would you feel if you were trying to study in a library and people were talking?

6. Jean is in a restaurant, and she remembers that she has to make a phone call. The call is important, and she can't wait. A man is using the one phone in the restaurant. Jean tries to get the man's attention. What does the man talking on the phone do? How does Jean feel?

7. Sandra has studied hard for a test with her friend Tanya. Sandra gets 75 on the test and Tanya gets 95. How does Sandra feel? How does Tanya feel?

8. Kevin promises to help Jason fix his bike after school. Jason waits and waits, and Kevin never arrives. How does Jason feel? The next day Kevin remembers his promise. How does he feel? What does he do?

Exercise 3   Make up two situations. Read them to the class. Ask the class how the people in the situations feel.

1. _____

   _____

   _____

   _____

   _____

2. _____

_____

_____

_____

_____

Exercise 4   Choose five emotions. Write a sentence that tells something about each one.

1. _____

2. _____

3. _____

4. _____

5. _____

Lesson 3   How Do You Feel?

Exercise 1   Answer the questions in complete sentences. The picture will tell you the answer.

Example: *Is the boy sad? Yes, he is,* or *No, he isn't. He's happy.*

1.   Is the lady tired?

_____

2.   Is the girl afraid?

_____

3.   Is the man sleepy?

_____

4.   Is the boy angry?

_____

Everyday English, Book Four

5. Is the baby happy?

_____

6. Is the boy worried?

_____

7. Is the woman surprised?

_____

8. Is the man confused?

_____

9. Is the man bored?

_____

10. Is the girl embarrassed?

_____

Exercise 2   Write a synonym for each of these words.

1. angry _____

2. happy _____

3. worried _____

4. sad _____

5. surprised _____

6. afraid _____

Exercise 3   Write an antonym for each of these words.

1. happy _____

2. afraid _____

3. worried _____

4. sad _____

5. sick _____

6. fine _____

Unit 1   Feelings and Emotions

7

Exercise 4   Complete the sentences with the correct words from the list at the right.

1. If you are sad, you want to _____ .

2. If you are happy, you want to _____ .   laugh

    help

3. If you are angry, you are _____ .   doctor

4. If you are afraid, you want _____ .   school

5. If you are sick, you want a _____ .   cry

    mad

6. If you are fine, you come to _____ .

Exercise 5   Write the name of an emotion in each box. For each situation the teacher describes, find the emotion and put an X over it. When you have five X's in a row you win the bingo game.

		FREE		

Everyday English, Book Four

Exercise 1   Complete the crossword puzzle. Write a synonym for each word across and an antonym for each word down.

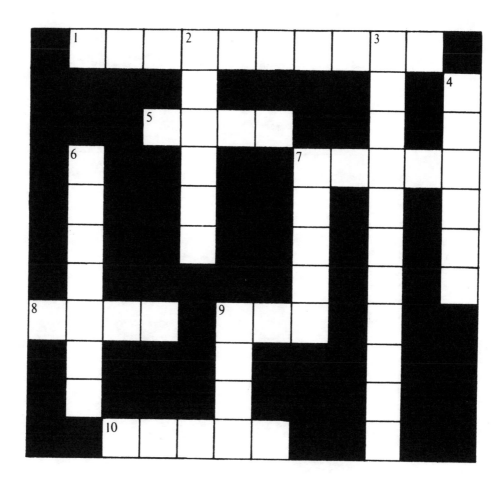

Across (Synonyms)

1 scared

5 love

7 unafraid

8 like

9 unhappy

10 sleepy

Down (Antonyms)

2 innocent

3 proud

4 awake

6 calm

7 interested

9 puzzled

Exercise 2   Find and circle the hidden words in the puzzle. The words to find are in the list below. The words may read across, down, or diagonally. They may be backward or forward. There are eight letters you will not use. They will spell what you studied in this lesson. Find them and write the mystery word below the puzzle.

frightened	sad	ill	like	guilty
angry	love	annoys	sleepy	bored
nervous	jealous	puzzled	feel	dislike
hate	hurt	dull	good	startled
detest	fly			

H	I	L	L	F	L	Y	R	G	N	A
E	A	Y	I	R	D	P	N	O	F	N
M	S	T	K	I	P	E	E	O	E	N
S	T	L	E	G	U	E	R	D	E	O
U	A	I	T	H	Z	L	V	O	L	Y
O	R	U	S	T	Z	S	O	T	B	S
L	T	G	E	E	L	S	U	R	O	L
A	L	T	T	N	E	A	S	U	I	O
E	E	U	E	E	D	D	O	H	N	V
J	D	S	D	D	I	S	L	I	K	E

Mystery Word: _____

Unit 2 After School

Lesson 5 Clubs

Exercise 1 Study the following dialogue.

Brenda: What do you do after school?

Will: Oh, nothing special.

Brenda: I'm going out with the bowling club. Would you like to come with me?

Will: That's a good idea. It sounds like more fun than staying home. Maybe I'll even join the team.

Brenda: Great! We meet every Monday from 3:00 to 5:00. I've made a lot of friends by joining the team. I don't feel alone anymore.

Will: Maybe I'll join something else, too: like the photography club or the track team. Thanks for thinking of me, Brenda. I appreciate it.

Brenda: I always like to help a friend.

Exercise 2 Write five questions about the dialogue.

1. _____

2. _____

3. _____

4. _____

5. _____

Exercise 3   Now answer the questions you wrote.

    1. _____

    2. _____

    3. _____

    4. _____

    5. _____

Exercise 4   Write a sentence for each word.

    1. bored _____

    _____

    2. club _____

    _____

    3. join _____

    _____

    4. bowling _____

    _____

    5. tournament _____

    _____

    6. basketball _____

    _____

    7. art _____

    _____

    8. swimming _____

    _____

    9. foreign language _____

    _____

    10. debating team _____

    _____

    11. track team _____

    _____

    12. photography _____

    _____

Everyday English, Book Four

Exercise 5   Visit one club at your school. Then answer these questions about the club.
Use complete sentences.

1. Where does the club meet? _____

_____

2. When does the club meet? _____

_____

3. How long is each meeting? _____

_____

4. How many people are in the club? _____

_____

5. Who leads the club? _____

_____

6. What did you do at the club meeting? _____

_____

7. Are any of your friends in the club? _____

_____

8. Did you make any new friends? _____

_____

9. Will you go back next week? _____

_____

10. Will you try another club next week? _____

_____

Lesson 6   At Home

Exercise 1   Read the dialogue.

(Raisa and Ahmed meet at lunchtime in the cafeteria.)

Raisa: My parents don't let me go out when I come home from
school. I finish my homework and then I'm bored.

Ahmed: How can you be bored? There are so many things to do at
home. You can read, write letters, watch TV, listen to the
radio, play music, paint, sew, or have friends come to visit.

Raisa: I know, but how can I stay home all the time? I want to <u>go to the park</u> or <u>visit the library</u> or just <u>see my friends</u> and <u>take a walk</u>.

Ahmed: Really, you should talk to your parents. Explain that they can trust you, and that you should be allowed to go out.

Raisa: I'll try, but I don't think it will help.

Ahmed: Good luck.

Exercise 2

Now read the dialogue again, changing the underlined words. Answer the questions about the dialogue.

1. Do you think Raisa will talk to her parents? _____

_____

2. Do you think they will change? _____

_____

3. Why or why not? _____

_____

4. Did Ahmed give good advice? _____

_____

Exercise 3

Complete the sentences. Write the correct letter on the line next to each number.

____ 1. My parents   a. to your parents.

____ 2. I want to go   b. don't trust me.

____ 3. Try to talk   c. watch TV and play music.

____ 4. I like to   d. to the library or the park.

Exercise 4

Answer the questions in complete sentences.

1. What do you do when you're at home? _____

_____

2. Do your parents give you enough freedom? _____

_____

3. What do they let you do? _____

_____

4. What do they forbid you to do? _____

_____

5. How do you help in the house? _____

_____

6. Do you think your parents understand you? _____

_____

Why or why not? _____

_____

7. Do you think you understand your parents? _____

_____

Why or why not? _____

8. Do you get along with your brothers and sisters? _____

_____

9. Are you jealous of anyone in the family? _____

_____

Why? _____

10. What would you like to do after school that you cannot do? _____

_____

_____

Lesson 7 At Night

Exercise 1 Match the antonyms.

_____ 1. dark   a. stand

_____ 2. empty   b. always

_____ 3. city   c. up

_____ 4. summer   d. inside

_____ 5. down   e. few

_____ 6. never   f. day

_____ 7. many   g. light

_____ 8. night   h. filled

_____ 9. outside   i. winter

_____ 10. sit   j. country

Exercise 2   Read the paragraphs.

When the sun goes down, the lights go on. The city never is dark. It is lit by lights of many kinds. There are streetlights, lights from signs, lights in houses, lights in skyscrapers, lights on cars.

As night comes, the streets are not empty. They are still filled with people. Many people are on their way to theaters and restaurants. Lines form outside movie theaters. On Friday and Saturday nights, many people are on their way to discotheques. In the summer, people fill the park to listen to concerts. Others sit at sidewalk restaurants and cafes. They eat, drink, talk, and watch the people who are passing by. There are many ways to spend the evening in the city.

Exercise 3   Write the words to complete the paragraph.

When the sun _____, the lights

_____ . The city never is _____ . It is

_____ by lights of many kinds. There are streetlights,

lights from _____ , lights in houses, lights in skyscrapers,

lights on _____ .

As night comes, the streets are not empty. They are still

_____ with people. Many people are on their way to

theaters and restaurants. Lines form outside _____ . On

Friday and Saturday nights, many people are on their way to

_____ . In the _____ , people fill the park

to listen to _____ . Others sit outside at sidewalk

restaurants and cafes. They eat, drink, talk, and _____

who are passing by. There are many ways to _____ the

_____ in the city.

Exercise 4   Answer the questions in complete sentences.

1. How does your city or town look at night?

_____

2. How is it different in the daytime?_____

_____

3. What can you do in your city or town at night?

_____

4. Are there any problems in your city at night?

_____

5. What do you do at night during the week?

_____

6. What do you do at night on the weekends?

_____

Lesson **8**   ## On the Weekend

Exercise 1   Read the paragraphs.

    Josh and Alicia find a lot to do on the weekends. Every Friday afternoon they do their homework. Every Friday night they go to a party with their friends. They dance all evening and come home very tired.

    Saturday mornings during the winter, Alicia has band practice, and Josh plays on the basketball team. In the summer they go to the park and play soccer with their friends. They have picnics and listen to concerts in the park. Sometimes there is a play instead of a concert. If they don't go to the park, they go to the beach. There they swim and lie in the sun. Saturday nights they go to a movie or a disco with their friends.

    On Sundays they go to museums, or go skating. In the summer they also may spend Sundays in the park or at the beach. They like fresh air. Sometimes they visit their relatives in other parts of the city. Sunday evenings they make sure all their homework is done, and they prepare what they need for school the next day. Josh and Alicia like the city, and they know how to have a good weekend.

Exercise 2   Look in the newspaper and find out what you can do on the weekend. Discuss what you found with the class. Choose one activity and do it. Then write about what you did.

_____

_____

_____

_____

_____

_____

_____

_____

_____

_____

_____

_____

_____

_____

_____

_____

_____

_____

_____

_____

_____

_____

_____

Everyday English, Book Four

Exercise 3   Compare your weekend and your weekday routines.

_____

_____

_____

_____

_____

_____

_____

_____

_____

_____

_____

_____

_____

_____

_____

_____

_____

_____

_____

_____

_____

_____

_____

Unit

3 The Telephone

Lesson 9   Alphabetizing

Exercise 1   Decode the secret message. You will use your knowledge of the alphabet to find the words. In the top box, write the letter of the alphabet that comes *two* letters before the letter in the bottom box. One word is filled in for you. If a bottom box is blank, write Z in the top box.

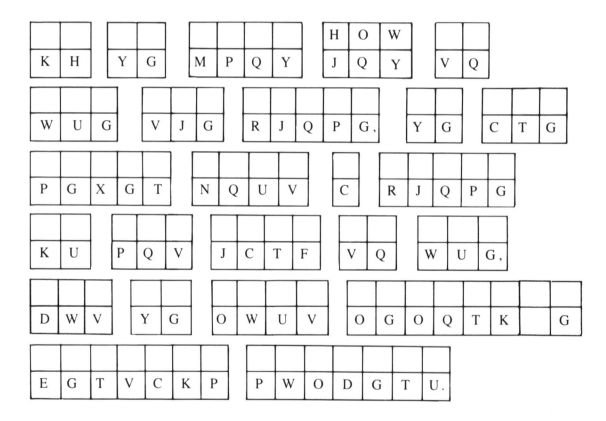

Exercise 2   Alphabetize means to put words in order by letters as they come in the alphabet. Alphabetize these words.

     snow   sell   shelf   ski   spot

     1. _____   4. _____

     2. _____   5. _____

     3. _____

Exercise 3   Alphabetize these words.

tame   table   taxi   target   tall

1. _____   4. _____

2. _____   5. _____

3. _____

Exercise 4   Alphabetize these words.

camel   came   camembert   camera   cameo

1. _____   4. _____

2. _____   5. _____

3. _____

Exercise 5   Alphabetize these names.

Slowik   Jong   Peterson   Rhee   Blake

1. _____   4. _____

2. _____   5. _____

3. _____

Exercise 6   Alphabetize these names.

Trudeau   Trufel   Trundel   Truong   Trubble

1. _____   4. _____

2. _____   5. _____

3. _____

Lesson **10** **More Alphabetizing**

Exercise 1   Alphabetize these words.

telephone   telegraph   telegram   telephoto

1. _____   3. _____

2. _____   4. _____

Exercise 2   Listen to your teacher and follow the instructions carefully.

1. _____   4. _____

2. _____   5. _____

3. _____

Exercise 3   Alphabetize these names.

Green, Betty   Green, Susan   Green, Karl
Green, Harvey   Green, Sidney

1. _____   4. _____

2. _____   5. _____

3. _____

Exercise 4   Alphabetize these names.

Brown, Joe N.   Brown, Joe W.   Brown, Joe B.
Brown, Joe D.   Brown, Joe H.

1. _____   4. _____

2. _____   5. _____

3. _____

Exercise 5   Listen to your teacher and follow the instructions carefully.

1. _____   4. _____

2. _____   5. _____

3. _____

Exercise 6   Alphabetize the following names. Then look for where they would come in
the phone book. Give the guide names on the top of the page where you
would find each name.

John Williams   Isabel Smith   Mai Lan
James Carres   Robert Perez

Name	Page	Guide Names
_____	_____	_____
_____	_____	_____
_____	_____	_____
_____	_____	_____
_____	_____	_____

Lesson **11** Area Codes and Special Numbers

Exercise 1   Study this information about telephones.

1. In the United States and Canada, *telephone numbers* have seven digits. For example, your number may be 555–4567.

2. Every telephone number also has an *area code*. This tells what part of the country the number is in. For example, an area code for Colorado is 303. Your friend's number in Colorado may be (303) 555–4567. If you call a number in your own area, you do not dial the area code. You only need area codes to dial *long distance*.

   To call *long distance*, dial 1, the area code, and then the seven-digit number you are calling.

3. If you don't have a *telephone directory* (book), dial 411 for information in your area.

4. For information outside your area, dial 1, the area code of the place you want, and 555–1212.

5. If you need help to make your call, dial *O* for *operator*.

6. If the area code is 800 before a number, that means the call is *toll-free*: it is a long-distance call that you don't have to pay for. Many businesses have numbers that begin with 800. To call an 800 number, dial 1, 800, and the seven-digit number.

Exercise 2   Study this area code map.

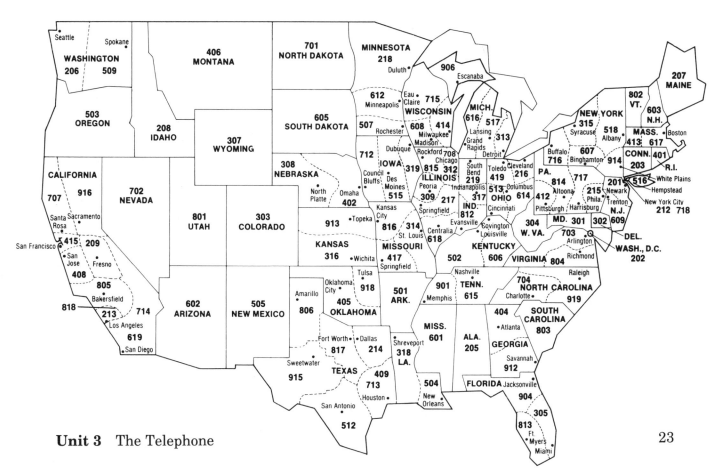

Unit 3 The Telephone

23

Exercise 3   Write the names of the states and cities that use the area codes given below. Refer to the map in exercise 2.

1. 609 _____   4. 212 _____

2. 415 _____   5. 319 _____

3. 305 _____

Now write the area codes for these places.

1. Arizona _____   4. New Orleans _____

2. New Mexico _____   5. Minneapolis _____

3. San Diego _____

Exercise 4   Write the phone numbers for these services in your city. Use your local phone book to find the numbers.

1. emergency _____   4. fire _____

2. police _____   5. weather _____

3. ambulance _____   6. time _____

Exercise 5   Complete the sentences.

1. Local means _____ .

2. Long distance means _____ .

3. Assistance means _____ .

4. Directory means _____ .

5. When you make a long-distance call, you must remember to first dial

_____ and then the _____ .

6. If you need help from the operator in your area, you dial _____ .

7. If you need to know a number in a different area code, you dial

_____ .

Lesson **12** Public and Home Phones

Exercise 1   Study the parts of a public phone.

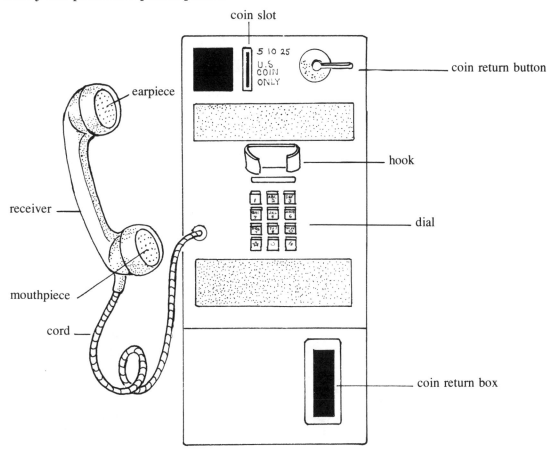

coin slot

5 10 25
U.S
COIN
ONLY

coin return button

earpiece

hook

receiver

dial

mouthpiece

cord

coin return box

Exercise 2   Now identify the parts of a home phone. Write the names on the lines.
Refer to exercise 1.

Exercise 3   Answer the questions in complete sentences.

1. What do you speak into and listen through? _____

_____

2. What do you hang the receiver on? _____

_____

3. Where do you put your money? _____

_____

4. What do you push if a coin gets stuck in the phone? _____

_____

5. Where does the money come out if no one answers and you hang up?

_____

6. What do you call the part of the phone that has the numbers and

letters written on it? _____

7. What attaches the receiver to the phone? _____

_____

8. How much does it cost to make a local phone call? _____

_____

9. What size coins can you put in the coin slot? _____

_____

10. Is there a coin slot on a private phone? _____

_____

Exercise 4   Unscramble these names for the parts of the phone.

1. v c i r e e r   _____

2. d o c r   _____

3. l a d i   _____

4. o k o h   _____

5. n o c i   l o t s   _____

Everyday English, Book Four

Lesson **13** Using the Telephone Book

Exercise 1   Study the following information.

1. The *telephone directory* is also called the *telephone book* or the *phone book.*

2. It has two major parts: the *white pages* and the *yellow pages.*

3. The *white pages* list everyone's name in alphabetical order.

4. Some people don't want their number in the phone book. They can have an *unlisted number.*

5. The *yellow pages* list numbers by types of businesses and services. For example, *dry cleaners* and *restaurants* are headings found in the yellow pages.

Exercise 2   Look in your local phone book, and find a name and number for each of these businesses or services. Write your answers on the lines.

1. dentists _____

2. drugstores _____

3. restaurants _____

4. travel agencies _____

5. movie theaters _____

Exercise 3   Look in your local phone book, and find the following numbers. Write your answers on the lines.

1. the post office _____

2. your school _____

3. a bank _____

4. the library _____

5. city hall _____

Exercise 4   Answer the questions in complete sentences.

1. When do you use the white pages?_____

    _____

2. When do you use the yellow pages? _____

    _____

3. Where can you find information about making telephone calls?

    _____

Exercise 5   Complete the sentences.

1. If you cannot find the information you want in the telephone book, you

   call _____ .

2. In your area, you dial _____ for directory assistance.

3. For directory assistance for another area, you dial _____

   _____ .

4. If you get a wrong number, you dial _____

   _____ .

Lesson **14**   Making a Phone Call

Exercise 1   Complete the dialogue.

*You want the operator to help you because you can't get the number
you want.*

Operator: May I help you?

You: _____

Operator: What number are you calling?

You: _____

Operator: One moment please. I'll try that number for you.

You: (to operator) _____

(The number rings and your friend answers.)

You: (to friend) _____

Friend: No, I didn't change my number. You must have dialed the
wrong number.

You: _____

Friend: Yes, I'd love to go to the beach this afternoon.

Exercise 2   Make up five questions about the dialogue.

1. _____

2. _____

3. _____

4. _____

5. _____

Exercise 3   Now answer the questions you wrote about the dialogue.

1. _____

2. _____

3. _____

4. _____

5. _____

Lesson **15** Review of the Telephone

Exercise 1   Answer the questions in complete sentences.

1. If you want to call your native country, what number do you dial?

   _____

2. If you call in your own area, do you use the area code? _____

   _____

3. What is the area code for your city? _____

   _____

4. What is the area code for the state north of you? _____

   _____

5. When you look for a name in the telephone book, do you look under the

   first name or the last name? _____

   _____

6. Which name comes first, Jones, John W. or Jones, John Y.?_____

_____

7. Do you get your money back when you dial 411 on a public phone?

_____

8. How many digits are there in a telephone number? _____

_____

Exercise 2   Complete the sentences.

1. On a public phone, you should listen for the dial tone before you put

   money into the _____ .

2. It costs _____ to make a local phone call.

3. You use the yellow pages to find _____ .

4. You use the white pages to find _____ .

5. The number for emergencies is _____ .

6. The number for local directory assistance is _____ .

7. The number for long-distance information is _____ .

8. A phone is important because _____

   _____ .

Everyday English, Book Four

Unit 4 The Library

Lesson 16 Getting a Library Card

Exercise 1   Match the words in column A with the definitions in column B.

	A		B
____	1. to take out		a. evidence
____	2. identification		b. must be returned
____	3. proof		c. or else
____	4. to apply		d. to take out again
____	5. due		e. to ask for
____	6. to renew		f. promptly
____	7. to return		g. to borrow
____	8. on time		h. a punishment that costs money
____	9. otherwise		i. to bring back
____	10. fine		j. proof of who you are

Exercise 2   Read the dialogue.

Pilar goes to the library to take out a book, but she doesn't have a library card.

Pilar: I'd like to take this book out, please.

Librarian: May I have your library card?

Pilar: I don't have one.

Librarian: You can't take out books without one.

Pilar: How do I get one? How much is it?

Librarian: It's free, but you must show some sort of identification with proof of your address. Do you have a driver's license or a student card?

Pilar: Here's my student card.

Librarian: Fill out this paper with your name and address. You may take out two books today. Come back next week for your card. The books are due in a month. If you're not finished by then, you can renew them for another month. Remember to return your books on time. Otherwise, you must pay a fine.

Pilar: Thank you.

Exercise 3   Answer the questions about the dialogue.

1. What does Pilar want to do? _____

   _____

2. Why can't she take out a book? _____

   _____

3. What does she need? _____

   _____

4. What does she show for proof of address? _____

   _____

5. How many books can she take out the first time? _____

   _____

6. When are the books due? _____

   _____

7. What can she do if she doesn't finish her books? _____

   _____

8. What happens if the books are overdue? _____

   _____

Exercise 4   Match the antonyms.

_____ 1. on time   a. to return

_____ 2. to have   b. unnecessary

_____ 3. important   c. to hide

_____ 4. to accept   d. incomplete

_____ 5. to show   e. last week

_____ 6. to come back   f. to reject

_____ 7. to take out   g. to cost

_____ 8. finished   h. late

_____ 9. to be free   i. to leave

_____ 10. next week   j. to need

Lesson **17** The Dewey Decimal System

Exercise 1   Read the sentences. Find a synonym from the list for each underlined word. Write the synonyms on the lines next to the sentences.

topic	organized	in the same place	labeled	nearly every
shows	important	sections	widely used	simple

1. There are books on <u>almost any</u> subject.   _____

2. The <u>subject</u> I like best is history.   _____

3. All libraries have three <u>divisions</u>.   _____

4. Each book is <u>marked</u> with a number.   _____

5. The number <u>indicates</u> the subject.   _____

6. The most <u>popular</u> system of classification
   is the Dewey Decimal System.   _____

7. Books are <u>classified</u> by subject.   _____

8. There are ten <u>major</u> divisions in the
   Dewey Decimal System.   _____

9. The same numbers are put <u>together</u> on
   the shelf.   _____

10. It's <u>easy</u> to use the library.   _____

Exercise 2   Read the paragraphs. Look for the words you studied in exercise 1.

You can find books on almost any subject in the library. All libraries have three large divisions: a general book collection, a magazine collection, and a reference section. Ask at the information desk if you have a question about where to find these sections.

Books on the same subject are grouped together: science books are all in one place, history books are all in one place, and so on. Each book is marked with a number. The number indicates the book's subject.

The most popular classification system today is the Dewey Decimal Classification System. There are ten major divisions in the Dewey Decimal System:

000–099	General Works
100–199	Philosophy
200–299	Religion
300–399	Social Science
400–499	Languages
500–599	Pure Science
600–699	Applied Science
700–799	Arts and Leisure
800–899	Literature
900–999	History

All books are put in order on the shelves by their numbers. This system makes the book you want easy to find. If you are looking for books on a subject but you don't know the name of a particular book, you know where to go. If you want a book on religion, for example, you know you must look in the 200s. Next time you go to the library, things will be easy for you to find.

Exercise 3   Answer the questions in complete sentences.

1. What are the three divisions in every library? _____

_____

2. How are the books in a library grouped? _____

_____

3. What do you find on each book? _____

_____

4. What is the name of the classification system used in most libraries?

_____

5. How is it divided? _____

_____

6. Which books go together on the shelves? _____

_____

7. What happens if you are looking for a subject but don't know the name
of any books on the subject? _____

_____

_____

8. What are the numbers of the Arts and Leisure section?

_____

9. Why will it be easy for you to use the library now? _____

_____

_____

_____

Exercise 4   What subjects are indicated by these numbers?

1. 653   _____

2. 960   _____

3. 085   _____

4. 427   _____

5. 342   _____

Exercise 5   Under what group of numbers can you find books on each of these subjects?

1. music   _____

2. World War I   _____

3. beginner's Spanish   _____

4. Moslem traditions   _____

5. poetry   _____

Exercise 1 Match the words in column A with their definitions in column B.

	A		B
____	1. title	a.	directions
____	2. author	b.	file
____	3. subject	c.	names
____	4. ancient	d.	writer
____	5. instructions	e.	box you can move
____	6. identifies	f.	major
____	7. drawer	g.	name of book
____	8. catalog	h.	very old
____	9. important	i.	find
____	10. locate	j.	topic

Exercise 2 Read the paragraphs. Look for the words you studied in exercise 1.

If you want to find a book in the library, you must know its number. In many libraries, you use a computer to find a book's number. In some libraries, you use a card catalog.

If you use a computer, you need to type information to help the computer locate the book. You should follow the instructions that the library has for typing information. If you use a card catalog, you look up information found on cards. A card catalog is a cabinet with drawers that contain cards. All the books in the library are listed on cards in the card catalog. The cards are in alphabetical order. If you see *ma–mo* on a drawer, you may find cards from *macrame* to *Mozart* inside.

Whether you use a computer or a card catalog, you look for books in the same way. You can look for books by *title, author,* or *subject.* You need to find the number that identifies the book.

If you want to find a book called *Ancient Egypt,* you need to look for the book by its *title.* In the card catalog, you would look under the letter *A.* This is the letter that begins the first important word in the title.

If you know that the author of the book about Egypt is James Bottari, but you don't know the title of the book, you need to look for the book by its *author.* You would look for the book by using the author's last name, *Bottari.* In the card catalog, you should look under the letter *B,* the letter that begins the author's last name.

If you're looking for a book about life in ancient Egypt, but you don't know the title or the author, look under the *subject*. The subject would be *Egypt*. Under that subject, you might find a number for the book *Ancient Egypt* by James Bottari.

In some card catalogs, there are separate files for the title cards, author cards, and subject cards. In other catalogs, all three kinds of cards are filed together.

If you see the word *Reference* in the information for a book, you may use the book in the library but you cannot take it home. Usually, you will find all the reference books together in one section of the library. Some common reference books are dictionaries and encyclopedias.

It is a good idea to talk with your librarian. The librarian will be able to help you find the books you want and tell you about special services in the library.

Exercise 3   Answer the questions in complete sentences.

1. What do you need to know to find a book in the library? _____

   _____

2. What can you use in libraries to find a book's number? _____

   _____

3. What does a card catalog contain? _____

   _____

4. If you know the name of a book, what do you look for to find its

   number? _____

5. If you know only who wrote the book, what do you look for to find its

   number? _____

6. If you know only the topic you want, what do you look for to find a

   book's number? _____

7. How is the reference section different from the other parts of the

   library? _____

8. Why is it a good idea to know your librarian? _____

   _____

Exercise 4   What would you use to look for each of the items — *title, author,* or *subject?*
Which letter must you look under in a card catalog?

	How to Look for Book(s)	**Letter**
1. a book named *History of Space Travel*	_____	_____
2. books by Alice Walker	_____	_____
3. *Life on the Mississippi*	_____	_____
4. a book named *Story of Mother Teresa*	_____	_____
5. books about sports	_____	_____
6. books by John Steinbeck	_____	_____
7. books about museums	_____	_____

Lesson 19   Kinds of Books

Exercise 1   Read the paragraphs.

In the library, there are two main kinds of books: fiction books and nonfiction books. Most libraries group fiction books in one area and arrange them in alphabetical order by the author's last name. Nonfiction books are put into a different area.

Fiction is something that is invented, or made up. An author has invented the events and people in fiction books. They come from the author's imagination. One important kind of fiction book is a novel. Novels tell stories. There are many kinds of novels. For example, science fiction novels usually tell made-up stories about life in the future or about life on other planets. Short stories, poetry, and plays are other kinds of fiction. Short stories are just what their name tells you they are. Poetry uses words and their sounds in special ways to create pictures and moods. Plays are stories to act out.

Nonfiction books are about real people and events. They report facts and things that really happened. For example, books on science, math, and history are nonfiction books. Biographies and autobiographies are nonfiction, too. Biographies are stories about people's lives. They are written by other people. Autobiographies are life stories that people write about themselves.

Most libraries also have a separate section for reference books. These are books such as encyclopedias and atlases. Encyclopedias contain articles about many subjects — about people, places, and things. The articles are in alphabetical order. Atlases are books of maps.

After you find the book you want in the library, you need to know how to use it. In the front of most nonfiction books, you will find a table of contents. This gives you the name of each chapter and the page number that it begins on. The table of contents lets you know what topics the book includes. At the back of a nonfiction book, there may be an index. The index is a long list of the subjects in the book. Next to each subject is the page number or numbers on which it is mentioned. An index is in alphabetical order.

Exercise 2   Answer the items in complete sentences.

1. What are the two main kinds of books? _____

   _____

2. How do many libraries arrange fiction books? _____

   _____

3. What is a fiction book? _____

   _____

4. Give an example of one kind of novel. _____

   _____

5. Give examples of three kinds of fiction. _____

   _____

6. Give two examples of nonfiction books. _____

   _____

7. What is a biography? _____

   _____

8. Name two kinds of reference books. _____

   _____

9. What do you find in a table of contents?_____

   _____

10. Where do you usually find an index? _____

   _____

Exercise 3　　Complete the sentences with the words from the list.

index	encyclopedia	invented	reference books
plays	table of contents	autobiography	biography
nonfiction	novels	fiction	atlas

1. Books in the fiction section are _____ .

2. If I write a book about Abraham Lincoln's life, it is a _____ .

3. If I write a book about my life, it is an _____ .

4. _____ are imaginary stories.

5. Math, science, and history are examples of _____ .

6. A book of maps is an _____ .

7. Stories to act out are _____ .

8. Short stories are an example of _____ .

9. Every book has a _____
to tell the pages the chapters begin on.

10. Encyclopedias and atlases are _____ .

11. An alphabetical list of subjects with the pages on which they can be

   found is the _____ .

12. A series of books that tells about almost every subject is an _____

   _____ .

Lesson 20　How to Write a Book Report

Exercise 1　　Study these instructions for writing a book report.

1. Give the title and the author.

2. Tell who or what the story is about. What are the names of the main characters? If the book is about a subject tell about the subject.

3. Tell when the story takes place.

4. Tell where it takes place.

5. Tell what happens to the main characters.

6. Tell if you liked the book.

7. Tell why you liked or did not like the book.

Exercise 2   Write a short book report. Use the list in exercise 1 to help you.

_____

by _____

_____

_____

_____

_____

_____

_____

_____

_____

_____

_____

_____

Exercise 3   Write a short book report at home. Use exercise 1 to help you.

_____

by _____

_____

_____

_____

_____

_____

_____

_____

_____

_____

_____

_____

Exercise 1   Complete the crossword puzzle.

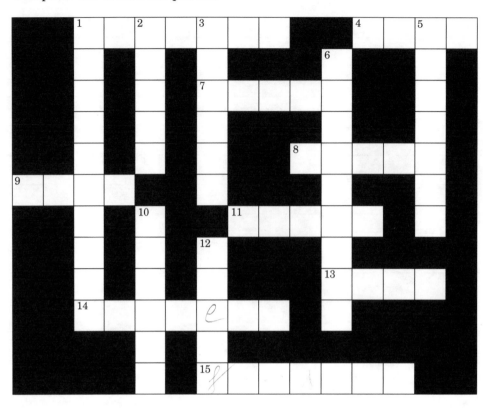

Across

1 You borrow books from the _____ .

4 If you are _____ , you must stay in bed.

7 There are three ways to find books in the library: by_____ , author, and subject.

8 If you want to find a book about steel, iron, gold, or silver, look for the subject _____ .

9 You need a library _____ to take out books.

11 The number classification system is the _____ Decimal System.

13 All the books in the library are listed in the _____ catalog.

14 If you don't know the author or the title, look under the _____ .

15 Books about invented stories are called _____ .

Down

1 People who work in the library are called _____ .

2 There are many _____ in the library.

3 If you know the writer, but not the name of the book, look under the name of the _____ .

5 You can find a book's identification number in the card _____ .

6 You may not take out books in the _____ section.

10 Every book has an identification _____ .

12 All books are arranged on a _____ .

Everyday English, Book Four

Unit

5 Sports

Lesson **22** Different Sports

Exercise 1   Match the pictures with the words. Write the correct word for each picture on the line.

soccer   football   baseball   tennis   volleyball

boxing   wrestling   swimming   basketball   hockey

1. _____
2. _____
3. _____
4. _____
5. _____

6. _____
7. _____
8. _____
9. _____
10. _____

Exercise 2   Match the pictures with the words. Write the correct word for each picture on the line.

ice skating   surfing   diving   skiing   sailing

bowling   sledding   bike riding   roller skating hiking

horseback riding   golf   racing   waterskiing   jogging

1. _____

2. _____

3. _____

4. _____

5. _____

6. _____

7. _____

8. _____

9. _____

10. _____

11. _____

12. _____

13. _____

14. _____

15. _____

Exercise 3   Unscramble the names of the sports. Then match each name to the correct picture. Write the correct name for each picture on the line.

c r o s c e   m w i g s i m n   l e a b l b s a
s i n n e t   n a l s i i g

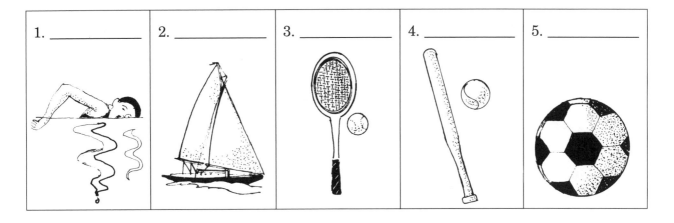

1. _____   2. _____   3. _____   4. _____   5. _____

Lesson 23   A Sport for Every Season

Exercise 1   Study the following chart.

Winter	Spring/ Summer	Fall	All Year	
ice skating	golf	football	horseback riding	bowling
skiing	baseball		soccer	swimming
sledding	sailing		tennis	hiking
ice hockey	waterskiing		boxing	roller skating
	surfing		volleyball	basketball
			bike riding	jogging
			racing	wrestling

Exercise 2   Match the season with the sport. You will use some letters more than once.

_____ 1. horseback riding   a. summer

_____ 2. sailing   b. fall

_____ 3. football   c. winter

_____ 4. golf   d. all year

_____ 5. skiing   e. spring

_____ 6. bowling

Exercise 3   Study these sentences. They tell about the places we play sports.

$$\text{We play} \begin{Bmatrix} \text{soccer} \\ \text{baseball} \\ \text{football} \end{Bmatrix} \text{on a } \textit{field.}$$

$$\text{We} \begin{Bmatrix} \text{ice-skate} \\ \text{roller-skate} \end{Bmatrix} \text{in a } \textit{rink.}$$

We ski on a *mountain.*

We surf on the *waves* in the *ocean.*

We bowl in a *bowling alley.*

$$\text{We play} \begin{Bmatrix} \text{tennis} \\ \text{volleyball} \\ \text{basketball} \\ \text{racquetball} \end{Bmatrix} \text{on a } \textit{court.}$$

We race around a *track.*

We swim in a *lake, ocean,* or *pool.*

People who play together form a *team.*

People who come to watch are called *spectators.*

People who like a sport are called *fans.*

Exercise 4   Name a sport for each place.

1. field   _____

2. rink   _____

3. court   _____

4. pool   _____

5. track   _____

Exercise 5   Write five sentences about your favorite sport.

_____

_____

_____

_____

_____

Everyday English, Book Four

Lesson **24** Equipment

Exercise 1   Identify the sport that the equipment shown is used for. Write the correct
word for each picture on the line.

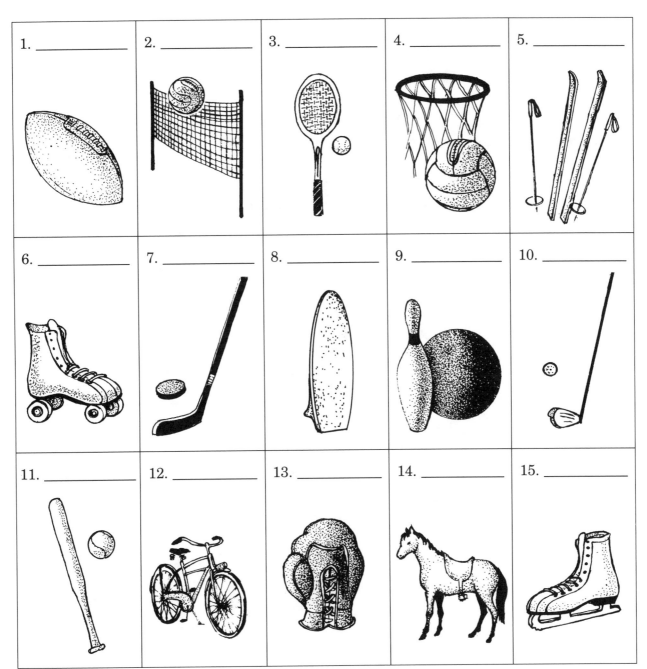

1. _____	2. _____	3. _____	4. _____	5. _____
6. _____	7. _____	8. _____	9. _____	10. _____
11. _____	12. _____	13. _____	14. _____	15. _____

Exercise 2   Complete each sentence with the name of the correct sport.

1. We wear gloves on both our hands when we _____ .

2. We hit the ball with a bat in _____ .

3. We use a ball and pins in _____ .

Unit 5 Sports   47

4. We use a big pointed ball in _____ .

5. We wear skates when we _____ .

6. We use a club and a tee when we play _____ .

7. We wear a bathing suit when we _____ .

8. We use a net when we play _____ .

9. We wear sneakers when we _____ .

Exercise 3   Answer the questions in complete sentences.

1. Where do you swim? _____

2. What sport do you use a racket for? _____

_____

3. What game do you use a club for? _____

_____

4. What game do you use a bat for? _____

_____

5. What is another name for running? _____

_____

6. When can you go skiing and ice skating? _____

_____

7. In what games do you hit the ball over a net? _____

_____

8. What sport takes place in a rink? _____

_____

Lesson 25 Review of Sports

Exercise 1   Complete the following sentences.

1. Football, soccer, and _____ are played on a field.

2. The people who come to watch sports are called _____ .

Everyday English, Book Four

3. We ice-skate in a _____ .

4. People who like a sport are its _____ .

5. People who play together form a _____ .

6. Two winter sports are _____ and _____ .

7. Two summer sports are _____ and _____ .

8. We play tennis on a _____ .

9. A sport in which two people fight is called _____ .

10. When you swim, you wear a _____ .

Exercise 2   Write the name of a sport that is related to each kind of equipment listed.

1. gloves _____   6. bat _____

2. basket _____   7. ice _____

3. snow _____   8. ball _____

4. pool _____   9. net _____

5. racket _____   10. skates _____

Exercise 3   Write a short composition about your favorite sport.

_____

_____

_____

_____

_____

_____

_____

_____

_____

_____

_____

_____

_____

_____

_____

_____

_____

_____

_____

_____

_____

_____

_____

Exercise 4   Unscramble the letters at left to find the names of sports. Write the words in the spaces at the right. Then unscramble the letters in the circles to find the answer to the mystery question.

n a i r g c

c o e s c r

g i s r e w t n l

a l y o e v l b l l

Mystery Question: When can we play these sports?_____

_____

Unit
6 The Newspaper

Lesson 26 The News

Exercise 1   Study this dialogue.

> **Janna:** I'm going to buy a newspaper. Come with me.
>
> **Phillip:** I don't read the newspaper.
>
> **Janna:** Why not?
>
> **Phillip:** Because the print is too small, and it makes my hands dirty.
>
> **Janna:** Those aren't good reasons. The newspaper is very important. You learn what's happening in the world.
>
> **Phillip:** I'd rather watch TV news.
>
> **Janna:** That's better than nothing, but you still learn more from a newspaper. There's a lot of extra information that you don't find on TV. I'll show you.
>
> **Phillip:** OK, tell me more.

Exercise 2   Answer the questions in complete sentences.

1. Where does Janna like to get her news?_____

_____

2. Where does Phillip like to get his news?_____

_____

3. Why is a newspaper better than the TV for news?_____

_____

Exercise 3   Watch the news on TV. Describe one important news item.

_____

_____

_____

_____

_____

_____

_____

_____

_____

_____

Exercise 4   Now look in the newspaper for the same news item. Answer the following questions.

1. Is the information in the newspaper the same as on TV? _____

_____

2. If there are differences, what are they? _____

_____

_____

3. Which report is more complete? _____

_____

4. Which report do you like better? Why? _____

_____

Lesson 27 News Publications

Exercise 1   Read the following paragraphs.

There are many different kinds of news publications. You can buy many different newspapers and magazines. They come out daily, weekly, or monthly.

There are several newspapers that are sold throughout the country. Almost every big city and small town has its own newspaper. In fact, large cities may have two or three newspapers. In these cities, there may also be community newspapers that tell about events in different parts of the city.

There are newspapers and magazines about business and politics and sports. There are newspapers and magazines about computers and movie stars. There are magazines and newspapers about almost every subject or activity you can think of.

Exercise 2

Go to the store or newsstand, and find the name of one of each of these types of news publications.

1. daily newspaper _____

2. newspaper sold nationwide _____

3. community newspaper _____

4. local magazine _____

5. business newspaper _____

6. sports magazine _____

7. news magazine _____

Exercise 3

News can be labeled or classified according to where it comes from. Match column A and column B.

A	**B**
____ 1. world	a. your country
____ 2. national	b. Arizona, Ohio, Florida
____ 3. metropolitan area	c. a city and the towns around it
____ 4. state	d. community
____ 5. local	e. different countries

Exercise 4

Find a headline for each type of news and write it on the lines.

1. world _____

_____

2. national _____

_____

3. metropolitan _____

_____

4. state _____

_____

5. local _____

_____

Read your headlines to the class and see if they can identify what kind of news they describe.

Lesson 28 Sections of a Newspaper

Exercise 1   A newspaper has many sections. Try to find out what each of the following sections contains. Write a short description of each. Discuss what you find with the class.

1. weather
2. editorial page
3. horoscope
4. comics
5. sports
6. entertainment

7. obituaries
8. classified section
9. want ads
10. international news
11. national news
12. state and local news

Exercise 2   List all the sections in your local newspaper.

_____

_____

_____

_____

_____

_____

_____

_____

_____

_____

_____

Lesson 29 More about the Newspaper

Exercise 1   Answer these questions. You may need to look for information in the library or ask someone who is familiar with American newspapers. Discuss the answers in class.

1. What is the press? _____

   _____

2. What is AP? _____

   _____

3. What is UPI? _____

   _____

4. What are reporters? _____

   _____

5. What are cub reporters? _____

   _____

6. What is a foreign correspondent? _____

   _____

Exercise 2   Explain the meaning of the following types of news. Again, you may need to do research or talk to people who know about newspapers. Discuss what you learn with the class.

1. objective news _____

   _____

2. subjective news _____

   _____

3. special features _____

   _____

4. topical news _____

   _____

Exercise 3   For each type of news in exercise 2, give an example from your local newspaper.

1. _____

   _____

2. _____

   _____

3. _____

   _____

4. _____

   _____

Exercise 4   Find an example of a news summary and an index in a newspaper. Use your examples to answer the following questions.

1. What are the major events in the news summary? _____

   _____

   _____

   _____

2. What is the value of this section? _____

   _____

   _____

   _____

3. What news do you want to read? _____

   _____

   _____

   _____

Everyday English, Book Four

Exercise 5   Answer these questions. You may need to look for information in the library or ask someone who is familiar with American newspapers. Discuss the answers in class.

1. What is an editor? _____

_____

2. What does an editor do? _____

_____

3. What is an editorial? _____

_____

Exercise 6   Read the editorial column in the newspaper. Write a letter to the editor.

_____

_____

_____

_____

_____

_____

_____

_____

_____

_____

_____

_____

_____

_____

_____

Exercise 7   Give your opinion. Answer these questions.

1. How do we decide if a paper is good or bad? _____

_____

_____

_____

2. How do we decide if the reporting is objective or subjective? _____

_____

_____

_____

3. What are some reasons that make it difficult for a paper to be

completely objective? _____

_____

_____

_____

4. What is our job as readers? _____

_____

_____

_____

Lesson **30** Review of the Newspaper

Exercise 1   Match column A and column B.

A	**B**
____ 1. headline	a. opinion
____ 2. obituary	b. beginners
____ 3. editorial	c. death notice
____ 4. comics	d. title of an article
____ 5. cub reporters	e. cartoons

Exercise 2   Write a sentence for each term.

1. objective _____

_____

2. opinion _____

_____

3. publish _____

_____

4. reporter _____

_____

5. special feature _____

_____

6. subjective _____

_____

7. UPI _____

_____

8. editor _____

_____

9. news index _____

_____

Exercise 3   Circle the correct choice to complete each sentence.

1. Advertisements tell about _____ .

   a. world news   b. sales   c. subjective news

2. AP stands for _____ .

   a. All People   b. Associated Press   c. Art Photography

3. The number of papers sold is called the _____ .

   a. deviation   b. presentation   c. circulation

4. The articles appear in _____ .

    a. columns   b. blocks   c. gates

5. A foreign correspondent is someone who _____ .

    a. writes strange   b. reports news from   c. is a native of a
       letters   another country   foreign country

6. An editorial is _____ .

    a. objective   b. subjective   c. always nasty

7. A deadline is _____ .

    a. a buried line   b. a due date   c. a broken wire

8. An editor _____ .

    a. owns the   b. mediates   c. chooses what is in
       newspaper   the newspaper

9. A headline _____ .

    a. tells the news   b. has wrinkles   c. is long
       in a few words

Exercise 4   How much do you know about the newspaper? Learn the meanings of these newspaper vocabulary words.

anchored articles _____

_____

by-line _____

_____

circulation _____

_____

copy _____

_____

critics _____

_____

floater _____

_____

format _____

_____

mass media _____

_____

masthead _____

_____

motto _____

_____

publication _____

_____

public relations _____

_____

publish _____

_____

publisher _____

_____

Appendix

The United States and Its Holidays

The United States

Exercise 1 Study this map of the United States.

Exercise 2   Read the information below as you look at the map. Discuss the italicized words with your teacher.

1. The United States is 3,000 miles wide.

2. There are fifty states in the United States.

3. Alaska is the biggest state.

4. Rhode Island is the smallest state.

5. Washington, D.C., is the *capital* of the United States.

6. We live in the state of _____ .

7. The capital of our state is _____ .

8. Canada is north of the United States.

9. Mexico and the Gulf of Mexico are south of the United States.

10. The Atlantic Ocean is east of the United States.

11. The Pacific Ocean is west of the United States.

12. People in America are of almost every *race, religion,* and *nationality.*

13. People from all over the world come to live in America.

14. Today there are over 247,000,000 people living in America.

15. English is the *official language,* but many other languages are spoken.

Exercise 3   Answer the questions in complete sentences. Refer to exercises 1 and 2.

1. Which state is the biggest? _____

_____

2. Which state is the smallest? _____

_____

3. Which state is the farthest northwest? _____

_____

4. Which state is the farthest northeast? _____

_____

5. Which state is the farthest southwest? _____

_____

6. Which state is the farthest southeast? _____

_____

7. Which two states are not next to the other states? _____

_____

8. Where is the Pacific Ocean? _____

_____

9. Where is the Atlantic Ocean? _____

_____

10. What country is to the north? _____

_____

11. What country is to the south? _____

_____

12. What is the capital of the United States? _____

_____

13. How large is the United States? _____

_____

14. How large is the population of the United States? _____

_____

Exercise 4   List the fifty states.

1. _____   10. _____

2. _____   11. _____

3. _____   12. _____

4. _____   13. _____

5. _____   14. _____

6. _____   15. _____

7. _____   16. _____

8. _____   17. _____

9. _____   18. _____

19. _____   35. _____

20. _____   36. _____

21. _____   37. _____

22. _____   38. _____

23. _____   39. _____

24. _____   40. _____

25. _____   41. _____

26. _____   42. _____

27. _____   43. _____

28. _____   44. _____

29. _____   45. _____

30. _____   46. _____

31. _____   47. _____

32. _____   48. _____

33. _____   49. _____

34. _____   50. _____

Exercise 5 Look at the pictures. Pronounce their names quickly, and see if you can guess which states they stand for. Write the correct state for each picture on the line.

5. _____

NEW + BRASS +

6. _____

7. _____

LOUISE + E + ANNA

8. _____

9. _____

FLOUR +

10. _____

+ AWAY

11. _____

MRS. HIPPY

12. _____

+ AH

13. _____

14. _____

Exercise 6   How many states have names that begin with each of the letters of the alphabet? Write the numbers under the letters. One has been done for you.

A	B	C	D	E	F	G
4						
H	I	J	K	L	M	N
O	P	Q	R	S	T	U
V	W	X	Y	Z		

Exercise 7   Alphabetize the states. Refer to exercises 4 and 6.

1. _____

2. _____

3. _____

4. _____

5. _____

6. _____

7. _____

8. _____

9. _____

10. _____

11. _____

12. _____

13. _____

14. _____

15. _____

16. _____

17. _____

18. _____

19. _____

20. _____

21. _____

22. _____

23. _____

24. _____

25. _____

26. _____

27. _____

28. _____

29. _____

30. _____

31. _____

32. _____

33. _____

34. _____

35. _____

36. _____

37. _____

38. _____

39. _____

40. _____

41. _____

42. _____

43. _____

44. _____

45. _____

46. _____

47. _____

48. _____

49. _____

50. _____

Exercise 8   Complete this map by filling in the names of the states.

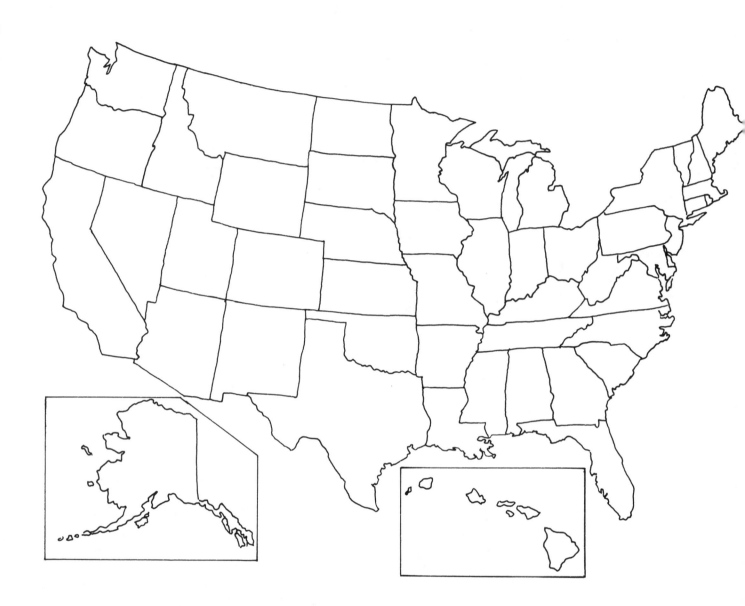

Everyday English, Book Four

Exercise 9   How much do you know about your native country? Answer these
questions.

1. Where is your country located? _____

    _____

2. What language do the people in your country speak? _____

    _____

3. What countries are to the north, south, east, and west of your country?

    _____

    _____

4. How large is your country? _____

5. What is its population? _____

    _____

6. What is its capital? _____

    _____

The Holiday Calendar

Exercise 1   Study the calendar. Some of these days are national holidays, and some of
them are special days that people enjoy celebrating.

January	**February**
1st—New Year's Day	14th—Valentine's Day
15th—Martin Luther King, Jr.'s Birthday (Celebrated the third Monday)	22nd—Washington's Birthday (Celebrated the third Monday)
March	**April**
	1st—April Fools' Day

May 30th—Memorial Day (Celebrated the last Monday)	**June**
July 4th—Independence Day	**August**
September First Monday—Labor Day	**October** 12th—Columbus Day (Celebrated the second Monday) 31st—Halloween
November First Tuesday—Election Day 11th—Veterans Day Fourth Thursday—Thanksgiving	**December** 25th—Christmas

Valentine's Day

Exercise 1   Match column A and column B.

A	B
____ 1. sweetheart	a. husband or wife
____ 2. custom	b. boyfriend or girlfriend
____ 3. festival	c. tradition
____ 4. to draw out	d. holiday
____ 5. mate	e. most of the time
____ 6. usually	f. to choose

Exercise 2   Read these paragraphs.

February 14 is a special day for honoring sweethearts. This custom is very old. It may go back to Roman times when a special festival called the "Lupercalia" was held on February 15. On that day, all young girls put their names in a box. Each young man drew out a name to pick his sweetheart for the next year.

During the Middle Ages, February 14 was the date when people believed birds found their mates. The day was set aside to honor all lovers. The people found new ways of celebrating the day. They used to kiss the "first-met," the first young woman they saw that day.

By chance, this special festival came on St. Valentine's Day. This day honors a Christian saint named Valentine. But the idea of honoring sweethearts has nothing to do with the saint the day is named for.

In the nineteenth century, the custom of sending valentines began. Valentines are pretty decorated cards or pieces of paper. These cards are sent to the people you care about the most. Today, Valentine's Day is very popular. People usually send valentines to many friends and relatives, not just to one person.

Exercise 3   Complete the sentences.

1. We celebrate Valentine's Day on _____ .

2. It is a day for _____ .

3. We send each other _____ today.

4. This custom of sending cards began in the _____ century.

Exercise 4   Answer the questions in complete sentences.

1. What was Valentine's Day called in Roman times? _____

   _____

2. How did the young men pick their sweethearts? _____

   _____

3. Whom does Valentine's Day honor? _____

   _____

4. What was the idea of *first-met?* _____

   _____

5. To whom do people send Valentine cards? _____

   _____

Is each sentence true or false? Write *true* or *false* on the line to the right of
each sentence.

1. Valentine's Day is a sad holiday.   _____

2. It is celebrated on February 15.   _____

3. This holiday honors sweethearts.   _____

4. We send cards to our sweethearts only.   _____

5. Valentine's Day is a very old celebration.   _____

George Washington's Birthday

Exercise 1   Read these paragraphs about George Washington.

George Washington was born on a plantation in Virginia on
February 22, 1732. There were no public schools in Virginia then, so
Washington studied at home. He liked to read, ride his horse, fish,
and hunt.

When Washington was eleven years old, his family moved to
Mount Vernon, Virginia. He became a surveyor and helped develop
frontier lands.

Washington was a courageous soldier. He became commander in
chief of the colonies' troops. On July 4, 1776, the colonies declared
their independence. In the war that followed, Washington led the
troops through many long and dangerous battles.

The United States was created after the war. This new country
decided to become a democracy. It wrote a constitution and elected a
president. The president was George Washington. He helped the
new country pay its debts and make laws for a democratic
government.

When he stopped working, Washington became a farmer and a
businessman. In December, 1799, he caught a bad cold and died soon
after. Every year we honor his memory with a national holiday on
February 22. Washington's picture is on every one-dollar bill and on
every quarter, and our nation's capital is named for him.

Exercise 2   Complete each sentence with the correct word from the list at the right.

1. A big farm is a _____ .

2. A country's basic laws are in its _____ .   constitution

                                                                  Mount Vernon
3. To catch seafood is to _____ .
                                                                  frontier
4. To measure land is to _____ it.
                                                                  courageous
5. A _____ is undeveloped land.
                                                                  plantation

6. Washington lived in _____, Virginia.

7. A free country is _____ .

8. If you owe someone money, you are in _____ .

9. A synonym for pick is _____ .

10. The United States was _____ in 1776.

11. A synonym for brave is _____ .

debt
fish
independent
survey
choose
created

Exercise 3   Arrange each group of words so that they make a complete sentence.

1. liked George to read Washington _____

_____

2. was brave Washington very _____

_____

3. at he home studied _____

_____

4. Virginia lived in he _____

_____

5. became he president _____

_____

Exercise 4   Is each sentence true or false? Write *true* or *false* on the line to the right of each sentence.

1. August 14 is Washington's birthday.   _____

2. Washington became commander in chief.   _____

3. He was a poor man.   _____

4. He was born in Louisiana.   _____

5. Washington's picture is on every penny.   _____

Exercise 5 Answer the questions in complete sentences.

1. Where was George Washington born? _____

_____

2. Where did he study? _____

_____

3. What did he like to do? _____

_____

4. Where did his family move to? _____

_____

5. How did Washington help the colonies? _____

_____

6. When did the colonies declare their independence? _____

_____

7. How did Washington help the new country? _____

_____

8. What did he do when he retired? _____

_____

9. How do we honor his memory? _____

_____

April Fools' Day

Exercise 1 Match column A and column B.

A	B
____ 1. trick	a. like a machine
____ 2. silly	b. mark
____ 3. spot	c. joke
____ 4. mechanical	d. stupid

Exercise 2   Read this paragraph about April Fools' Day.

On April 1, you can play silly tricks on your friends. For example, some people put mechanical mice in a drawer or say that there's a spot on your face when there really isn't. When the trick is finished, the person says "April Fool." It is a day when many crazy things can happen.

Exercise 3   Answer the questions in complete sentences.

1. What are some examples of silly things to do on April Fools' Day?

   _____

   _____

   _____

2. Do you have such a day in your country?

   _____

3. What is the name of the day?

   _____

4. How do you celebrate it?

   _____

Memorial Day

Exercise 1   Match column A and column B.

A	B
____ 1. graves	a. remembrance
____ 2. memorial	b. most likely
____ 3. origin	c. custom
____ 4. tradition	d. tombs
____ 5. probably	e. roots

Exercise 2   Read these paragraphs about Memorial Day.

At first, Memorial Day honored the soldiers who died in the Civil War. It is thought that a woman of French origin started this tradition. She probably chose May 30 because that day was the French Memorial Day.

Today it honors soldiers who died in all wars. It is a legal holiday. It is now celebrated on the last Monday in May. Schools, banks, and post offices are closed. There are military parades and memorial programs. People decorate graves of soldiers with flowers and little American flags. Many people think of Memorial Day as the official start of the summer season.

Exercise 3   Answer the questions in complete sentences.

1. When is Memorial Day now celebrated? _____

_____

2. Whom does it honor? _____

_____

3. When did it begin? _____

_____

4. How do we celebrate it today? _____

_____

5. Why was May 30 chosen? _____

_____

6. Does Memorial Day honor only Civil War veterans? _____

_____

7. What is a veteran? _____

_____

8. What happens on a legal holiday? _____

_____

Exercise 4   Do some research. Find out how Memorial Day is celebrated in your city.
You may want to talk to people to get information or look in old
newspapers. Discuss what you learn with the class.

_____

_____

_____

_____

_____

_____

_____

_____

_____

_____

_____

_____

_____

Independence Day (The Fourth of July)

Exercise 1   Match column A and column B.

	A		**B**
____	1. independence		a. declare
____	2. proclaim		b. celebrate
____	3. legal		c. types
____	4. observe		d. freedom
____	5. kinds		e. official

Exercise 2   Read the following paragraph.

> July 4 is America's birthday. On this day in 1776, the
> Declaration of Independence was proclaimed. The thirteen colonies
> no longer belonged to England. Philadelphia was the first city to
> observe this holiday. People rang the church bells, played music, and
> listened to a reading of the Declaration of Independence. In 1941,
> July 4 became a legal holiday. In most cities today, there are
> fireworks, picnics, and parades, and many businesses close. It is one
> of the most fun days of the summer.

Exercise 3   Answer the questions in complete sentences.

1. What does July 4 celebrate? _____

_____

2. What was the first city to observe this holiday? _____

_____

3. How did the people of Philadelphia celebrate July 4? _____

_____

4. When did it become a legal holiday? _____

_____

5. How is it celebrated today? _____

_____

Exercise 4   Tell how your city celebrates July 4. Find out how other parts of the
United States celebrate this holiday.

_____

_____

_____

_____

_____

_____

_____

_____

Labor Day

Exercise 1   Match column A and column B.

	A		B
____	1. organization	a.	start
____	2. establish	b.	period
____	3. ever since	c.	from then on
____	4. season	d.	finished
____	5. over	e.	group

Exercise 2   Read this paragraph about Labor Day.

> The Knights of Labor, a workers' organization, established this holiday in New York City in 1882. It was felt that working people should be honored. The group held a big parade. In 1887, the United States Department of Labor declared the first Saturday in June a legal holiday. In 1893, Labor Day was changed to the first Monday in September, and it has been that way ever since. This holiday also marks the official end of summer. Schools usually open later in the week.

Exercise 3   Answer the questions in complete sentences.

1. Who started Labor Day? _____

   _____

2. Why did this organization establish Labor Day? _____

   _____

3. How was it celebrated then? _____

   _____

4. When did it become a legal holiday? _____

   _____

5. When was the day changed to the first Monday in September? _____

   _____

6. What else does the holiday mark? _____

   _____

7. What opens soon after Labor Day? _____

_____

8. Do you have Labor Day in your native country? When is it? _____

_____

Columbus Day

Exercise 1   Write a sentence for each word.

1. boats _____

2. sea _____

3. sailors _____

4. quick _____

5. spices _____

6. supplied _____

7. discovered _____

8. believed _____

9. trip _____

10. started out _____

Exercise 2   Read these paragraphs about Columbus.

Christopher Columbus was born in Italy in 1451. He always loved boats and the sea. When he grew up, he became a sailor and moved to Portugal. Columbus wanted to reach Asia by sailing west. He thought that the earth was round, and that if he sailed west, he would find a shorter route to India. It was very important to find a quick route to the Orient to bring back the valuable spices and silks that the Europeans liked.

Queen Isabella and King Ferdinand of Spain supplied Columbus with three ships: the *Niña,* the *Pinta,* and the *Santa María.* In August 1492, he started out on his trip. On October 12, 1492, he reached the Bahamas. He called the people there Indians because he believed he was in India. He sailed on and discovered Puerto Rico, Cuba, and Hispaniola, the island shared by Haiti and the Dominican Republic.

Everyday English, Book Four

We celebrate Columbus Day with a parade and a legal holiday. Schools and banks are closed. If there is a parade in your town, go and see it.

Exercise 3   Answer the questions in complete sentences.

1. When was Columbus born? _____

_____

2. What did he always like? _____

_____

3. What did Columbus dream of? _____

_____

4. What did he think? _____

_____

5. Why was it important to find a quick route to the Orient? _____

_____

Exercise 4   Is each sentence true or false? Write *true* or *false* on the line to the right of each sentence.

1. Queen Elizabeth supplied Columbus with three planes.   _____

2. He left on his trip in August 1492.   _____

3. His three ships were the *Niña*, the *Pinta*, and the *Santa María*.   _____

4. He first arrived in the Bahamas.   _____

5. He called the people Indians because he watched a lot of westerns on TV.   _____

6. He also discovered Cuba, Puerto Rico, and Hispaniola.   _____

7. Columbus Day is a legal holiday.   _____

Halloween

Exercise 1   Match the pictures with the words. Write the correct word for each picture on the line.

corn   pumpkin   ghost   witch   skeleton

bat   owl   black cat   jack-o'-lantern scarecrow

1. _____

2. _____

3. _____

4. _____

5. _____

6. _____

7. _____

8. _____

9. _____

10. _____

Exercise 2   Read these paragraphs about Halloween.

In England thousands of years ago, the people celebrated *Summer's End*. They thanked the sun for the good harvest. They decorated their huts with fruits and vegetables, such as apples, corn, and pumpkins. Scarecrows in the fields kept the birds from eating their crops.

Even more exciting was the evening before, Halloween. On this night people thought that ghosts and witches, black cats, bats, and owls came. The people believed in ghosts and witches. They built fires on the mountains to keep them away.

Today, on October 31, children put on masks. They go from house to house and say "Trick or Treat." Everyone gives them candy, so they don't play tricks. Adults and children often put on costumes and go to Halloween parties. People enjoy carving pumpkins to make jack-o'-lanterns for Halloween.

Exercise 3   Complete the sentences.

1. In England, people had a celebration called _____ .

2. They thanked the _____ for a good _____ .

3. The evening before was called _____ .

4. On this night _____ and _____ came.

5. The people made big _____ to scare the _____ .

Exercise 4   How do we celebrate Halloween today?

_____

_____

_____

_____

_____

Exercise 5   Look at the pictures and complete the sentences.

1. The _____ is riding a broom.

2. The _____ is a night bird.

3. A _____ flies at night, too.

4. The black _____ is a symbol of Halloween.

5. We carve pumpkins to make _____ .

Election Day

Exercise 1 Read these paragraphs about Election Day.

The United States is a democracy. The people choose the U.S. president and vice-president, state governors, city mayors, and all other government leaders.

Election Day is always on the Tuesday after the first Monday in November. Many people go to the polls to vote. There are two major parties in the United States: the Democratic Party and the Republican Party. There are many other smaller parties.

What positions will be filled in the elections in your state this year? You can vote if you are an American citizen and are at least eighteen years old.

Exercise 2 Complete the sentences.

1. Democracy means that _____ .

2. The Tuesday after the first Monday in November is _____

_____ .

3. The two major parties are _____

_____ .

4. This year we elect _____

_____ .

5. Every American citizen who is at least _____
   years old may vote.

Exercise 3   Answer the questions in complete sentences.

1. Is the United States a democracy? _____

   _____

2. How many major parties are there? _____

   _____

3. When is Election Day? _____

   _____

4. Where do the people go to vote? _____

   _____

Veterans Day

Exercise 1   Match column A and column B.

A	B
____ 1. armistice	a. former soldier
____ 2. veteran	b. burial ground
____ 3. ally	c. official events
____ 4. ceremonies	d. truce
____ 5. cemetery	e. friend

Exercise 2   Read these paragraphs about Veterans Day.

   Veterans Day used to be called "Armistice Day." It celebrated the end of World War I, November 11, 1918. On that day the Allies and the Germans signed an armistice, or a peace. After World War II, Armistice Day also honored soldiers who served in that war. In 1954, after the Korean War, President Eisenhower changed the name of the holiday to "Veterans Day," in honor of all the veterans of all the wars.

   We celebrate this holiday with parades, speeches, and by placing flowers on the graves of soldiers. There are special ceremonies at the Tomb of the Unknown Soldier in Arlington National Cemetery near Washington, D.C. Banks, schools, and post offices are closed for the day.

Exercise 3   Complete the following sentences.

1. The original name for Veterans Day was _____ .

2. The end of World War I happened _____ .

3. In _____ , the name of the holiday was changed to

_____ .

4. Today it honors _____ .

5. We celebrate the day with _____ .

Thanksgiving

Exercise 1   Match the pictures with the words. Write the correct word for each picture
on the line.

Pilgrim	ship	basket	cider
catching fish	deer	corn	berries
clam	pumpkin pie	Indian	turkey

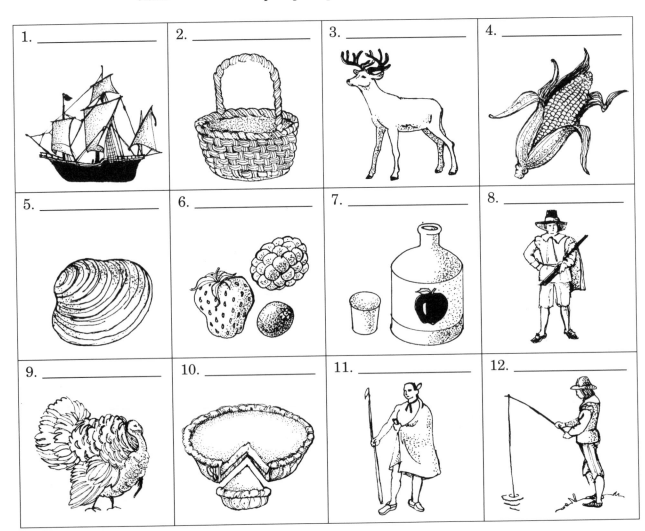

1. _____
2. _____
3. _____
4. _____
5. _____
6. _____
7. _____
8. _____
9. _____
10. _____
11. _____
12. _____

Everyday English, Book Four

Exercise 2   Read about the first Thanksgiving.

In November 1620, the Pilgrims landed in America. They were cold, tired, and sick from their long trip across the Atlantic Ocean in their ship, the *Mayflower*. They needed houses, so they went to work and cut down trees. The winter was very cold. As a result, many of the Pilgrims died before the summer came. Their food was almost gone.

Luckily, friendly Indians showed them how to catch fish and clams, and showed them where to hunt for deer. Most important of all, the Indians showed the Pilgrims how to plant corn, a new food for these Europeans.

In the fall, the Pilgrims harvested their corn crop. They filled baskets with vegetables, and more baskets with corn for the coming winter. The Pilgrims were happy and decided on a special day to give thanks for their good fortune. The Indians joined them, and they ate together at long wooden tables. They ate turkey, venison (deer meat), clams, fish, corn bread, cranberry sauce, and many fruits and vegetables. "Thanksgiving," as they called it, became a tradition, and when Abraham Lincoln became president, he made it a holiday for the whole country. Today, Thanksgiving is celebrated every year on the fourth Thursday in November.

Exercise 3   Answer the questions in complete sentences.

1. Who were the Pilgrims? _____

   _____

2. When did the Pilgrims come to America? _____

   _____

3. What was the name of their ship? _____

   _____

4. Who helped the Pilgrims? _____

   _____

5. How did they help the Pilgrims? _____

   _____

Exercise 4   Is each sentence true or false? Write *true* or *false* on the line to the right of each sentence.

1. The Pilgrims' first harvest was very poor.   _____

2. The Pilgrims decided to have a special
   day to give thanks.   _____

3. They invited the King of England.   _____

4. They ate hamburgers.   _____

5. Abraham Lincoln declared Thanksgiving
   a national holiday.   _____

Exercise 5   Complete the sentences.

1. The Pilgrims came to America in the year _____ .

2. The name of their ship was the _____ .

3. The winter was _____ .

4. The _____ helped the Pilgrims.

5. They showed them how to _____

   _____ .

6. They taught the Pilgrims about a new food called _____ .

7. In the fall, the Pilgrims _____ their corn _____ .

8. The Pilgrims decided to _____ .

9. They invited the _____ to join them.

10. They ate _____ .

11. President _____ declared _____
    a national holiday.

Exercise 6   What are you thankful for this year?

_____

_____

_____

_____

_____

_____